To the memory of my mother and father
Alma and Vernon

Acknowledgments

The author is grateful to the editors of the following publications in which these poems, or versions of them, first appeared: *Cumberland Poetry Review; Iowa Woman; Isthmus; Kentucky Poetry Review; Native Lumber; Piedmont Literary Review; Poet Lore; Poetry Ireland Review; Primipara; Transactions; Wisconsin Poetry; Wisconsin Poets' Calendar 1986.*

Some poems in this collection appeared in the chapbook, *The Sun Rides in Your Ribcage*, Fireweed Press, 1987.

Special thanks to the Wisconsin Arts Board for a fellowship supporting work on this collection; to the Tyrone Guthrie Centre at Annaghmakerrig, Ireland, where several of these poems were completed; and to my manuscript groups in Wisconsin and Dublin.

And, as always, thanks to Tom, who helps me get closer to what I mean to say.

When It Came Time

Jeri McCormick

Salmonpoetry

Published in 1998 by
Salmon Publishing Ltd,
Cliffs of Moher, Co. Clare

© Jeri McCormick 1998   1|6|00
The moral right of the author has been asserted.

A catalogue record for this book is available from the British Library.

The Arts Council   Salmon Publishing gratefully acknowledges the
An Chomhairle Ealaíon financial assistance of The Arts Council.

ISBN 1 897648 05 7 Softcover

Cover design by Brenda Dermody
Cover artwork by Austin Carey
Set by Siobhán Hutson
Printed by Betaprint, Clonshaugh, Dublin 17

The Appalachians present the melancholy spectacle of a people who have acquired civilization and then lost it.

Arnold Toynbee, historian

Root hog or die.

frontier maxim

Though I live not where I love.

Irish emigrant song

Contents

The Arrival

I station myself
in your doorway,
a hobo bundle
with stiff knot
and shifting load.

I have arrived
with long rosters
and hard accumulations,
the heavy shadow
of your former self.

I am your history,
tattered and abiding
as a poor relation.

You will have to take me in.
I know too much.

When It Came Time

Kentucky's brooding hills
were stripped of futures
though the older folks held on,
digging, planting, watching
the brown river cover their corn.
Even the mines had darkened
their black doors and trains
along the bottom were few.

Father had left years earlier
to tend a war-boom lathe
twelve hours a night
six nights a week.

Now a young cousin
would migrate too,
forsaking spring mud
and the mule-drawn plow.

At his farewell supper
Aunt Edna served chicken
in lard can lids and we sat
on the porch among dogs and stars.
In morning darkness each took a turn
at the privy and Ray Neal packed
his belongings in a brown paper sack.

We waited in the Nash while he
hugged his hulking dad and tearful mom,
kissed his older sister and ragged brother,
held the puppy one last time.

Riding northward in silence,
watching dawn's mist
abandon hillsides,
we saw summits flatten
to a gray linear band
beneath the lowering sky.

On humming wheels we reached
the massive bridge, its beams and cables
framing Ohio's Queen City, underscoring
Carew Tower's steel thrust.
Below, barges were coming to rest
at concrete banks.

Ray Neal leaned forward
and we leaned with him,
first time travellers again
forgetting for a moment
departure's grief, arrival's
apprehension, all the rest

that would come. We gave ourselves
to crossing. We gave ourselves
to the wide span of wonder.

Rails

The mountains stand quietly sufficient,
lifting their waft of sky like broadcloth

across the Cumberland where residents
advance daily purpose in slanted fields

as did their ancestors, send their children
to skip on footbridges and hide in bottom corn,

my father among them, a boy in pinned-up
overalls feeding the hogs and pondering

the wider world his schoolmaster speaks of,
though he hears there are neighbours enough

to wonder about down his own mountain's
twisting hollow, upriver in the next raised

kingdom. The stories he shares with cousins
in the dusk air, swings with on lazy porches,

are the old ones – heroes and ghosts that weave
their derring-do into family. But the Outside

has its agenda and by 1912 the first long noise
on iron wheels zigzags along misty slopes,

chasing rivers, calling out dreamers who've paced
the wooden ties that lead to Somewhere Else,

and the engineer looks out from speed and status
to wave at the wondering folk on hillsides

as he huffs his line of Lexington & Eastern
gondolas on down to the pyramid of luminous black

hacked from the hunched earth by hirelings who
give up the slow, sweet hours of day in exchange

for a new century's murky promise, deep, deep,
where the tiny finch releases its flickering song.

4

Lineage

Retirement sent our Dexter forth
to track the lines of family,
his careful fingers skimming across
Kentucky's frayed history – writs of boundary
scalping the Shawnee; eight generations of nuptials,
deaths, births, peopling
the Commonwealth.

Dexter braved all that, sure
of our place in the old forest
Boone had coveted, tracing us
eastward to the source – that tattered
vision at Valley Forge where Elder James,
our own founding father, tended his
frostbitten toes, too besieged to ponder
his part in nation-building

or see how a Welsh-deep dream might rise
like mist from the banks of the Delaware
to settle beyond the Gap; how a mountain
might stand as paycheck, high legal tender
for a ragtag soldier who'd never been
to Kentucky; how he'd end up
taking us all there.

Miners' Morning

From hillside porches they emerge
in firefly hats with carbide glow –
fathers, brothers, sons, who breathe
the river's mist and walk the rail-
road ties, a squadron of phantoms
who cross the dark bottomland to face

the chilling descent they'd never choose
if miners believed in choices.

Deep inside their shafts, the miners
forego Kentucky's curve of morning,
its warm ministrations that wake
the wrens, the willows, the common
blades of grass. For those encased
in coal's hard cycle, day itself
has dropped to dusky hearsay.

A Country Childhood

Born to a landscape
of furrowed progressions
I met Earth in spring
at the start of its hum.
Life was new as the chicks
in Aunt Kate's incubator
old as the terrapin
in Tim Blevins' pond.

I rode the barnyard gate
inhaling morning clouds,
stood at the back door stoop
dazzling the Big Dipper.

I learned what all kids learn in such places:
how the orchard stands by while you nap,
the pear trees waiting
like diligent playmates;
how the woodshed hides a cousin
holding for you a deafening 'boo';
how the corn whispers your name
as you file among its green ensigns;
how a daisy chain is like a day
encircling you in time and space.

I watched many hands
advance that rooty system,
saw fewer continue
when war hauled off the uncles.

That was decades ago.
What remains to geography
is a sparser county, a corporate presence;
what remains for me
is an intimate history
snug as a featherbed's dream.

Journey

At Somerset and Buncombe and Danville
the train stops, collects the shabby
standing with cardboard grips, buttoned-up
faces – I see this in sepia now – Kentucky
of 1940 slipping along our windows: snow-
dusted hills, bronze-leafed woods, fields
abandoned by red-knuckled farmers gone in

to wood fires and newspapers rattling of
far-off war while November's brown mouth
swallows track as we leave it, inhales our
engine's steam, and we become a long noise
rattling our way on a workers' pilgrimage,
past the make-believe of Lexington, Daddy
pointing to white fences, silk-sleek horses,

Mother turning from the baby to the splendid
houses, the sun streaming its gold around
us, a sign I believe – *we're going to get
rich* – but nightfall erases all, releases
stale air, the window becomes mirror-hazed,
disembodied faces in passing trains, babies
crying until at last Daddy says 'It's the river'

and takes me on his knee to see the bridge,
so long a crossing, soft sheen on black water
then the lights – lights stunning the windows,
climbing and dropping, glowing and flashing,
puncturing the high bank of darkness, dabs of
sparkle rising to a fixed restlessness, merging
into a luminous pall: Ohio, the next galaxy.

My Mother's Guitar

The gleam of varnish,
   the long fretted neck,
      the painted rose, throb-red,
         thorn-driven as she was –
            I see this fifty years after
              she snapped the case

and carried her music up
   to Grandma's mountain attic,
      our lives waiting below
         like laid-out strings
            unattached, none of us knowing
              what would come next,

who we'd become, how much
   we'd miss my mother's untutored
      tunes in the discordant city.
         Radio brought the Grand Ole Opry,
            Music Hall booked Roy Acuff,
              but we'd never again hear

my mother's lament for Clementine
   nor her finger-flying version of
      'Wabash Cannon Ball,' a few lines
         hummed when the words fell
            off track; and though she made
              us a home in Cincinnati's clamour,

pointing us down the streets
   we'd have to take, leading us
      to other instruments, other songs,
         she never again opened the coffin case,
            never again rested the guitar's
              wooden hip against her own.

Sentinel

Back at the house the grownups gather
to talk of Hitler, the walls reflecting
pale circles from oil lamps, the clock
swinging its unconcerned pendulum,

the room's only child pondering a sky
she'd not seen before – shifting poles
of light over the darkened fields, surely
the world coming to an end, she thinks,

Behold, he cometh with clouds; but she
says nothing and the crickets
continue their loud accompaniment,
all kindreds of the earth shall wail.

She studies faces, listens for the
thunder that will clap them to the lap
of Jesus where they'll sit forever looking
at lambs, *a little child shall lead* . . .

'Sweet dreams' everyone says, she goes
dutifully to bed, beset by war and
Sunday School; then Daddy bends to ask
did she see the search light, like a giant

flashlight beaming across Pulaski County.
Sleep will spread its quilted comfort,
she knows, but first there is the window,
the sorting of its scrambled stars.

The Night of No Talking

We walked along the orchard's edge,
Grandma holding the lantern,
the aroma of pears sweetening our hair,
our destination a hump of hillside,

the neighbour's window embedded there
like a grounded star. The kingdom
we passed through belonged to
nightfall musicians – crickets and frogs

keening their compositions.
I composed a sheaf of questions,
child-sized, kept them folded
like good Sunday handkerchiefs.

The woman who met us at the stoop,
eyes flat as worn pennies,
stationed me in a stiff chair,
led Grandma to the next room,

a society of whispers. Long minutes,
then the door's creaking exposure:
table in dim light, bare arms and legs,
a glimpse of fan-patch quilt,

Grandma washing feet, blue-tinged, old.
Rush of footsteps. Click of latch.
The window near me an open mouth inhaling,
lifting the curtain's gauzy hem.

Later, in the mist-draped air,
the Big Dipper poured its silver elegy
along our path and Grandma switched
the lantern to take my hand.

Making Room

Going to bed
she climbed into her thumb
as usual, but dreams that night
flashed Rumpelstiltskin
stamping and shrieking.

She woke with the mourning dove
and Grandma Whitaker calling
her in to Mother's bed.
Daddy danced her over
to a small blue blanket

and she looked inside
at a rubber-ball head,
toy feet and fingers.

So this was it.

She went back to bed
to wait for her breakfast,
the mourning dove flew off

to meet the day and by the time
the hot cakes were ready
she had gathered up her things –

book of Grimm's tales, green
Sears tricycle, old tire swing

and packed them all
with quick, dire ceremony
into the warm velvet lining
of her thumb.

Cherries and Choices

She pinches
Little Brother

sweats it out
in the pantry

Mother slips in
to tell about Hell

and line up
the pickle jars.

At lesson's end
she studies the canned

tomatoes, swaggers
on out to her cherry tree,

suspended
between wings and horns,

the hours smouldering by.
At suppertime

she scurries down
in juice-pocked dress

bare feet quick
on the hot pitted path.

A Fable for Rain

When mountain people killed a black snake,
they would hang it in a bush so that rain would come.
  Memoirs of Custer Back

Each limp spectacle
draped among the laurel
catches the Lord's nostalgic eye,
calling up the Eden serpent –
that consummate villain.

Who could forget
the graceful tilt
of slender head,
the intimate, rakish smile,
the artful pitch to Eve
in beguiling sunlight?

God applauded in secret
that day, far from the mortal
pair He'd had to chastise.
Even the elder angels smiled,
knowing the burden of Knowledge
would finally be shared;
Earth would be uniquely spared
perfection's ripe monotony.

And so the slain descendent,
slung in the bushy fate
of betrayer/betrayed,
bathes in commemorative tears,
glistens in a downpour of Grace.

First Christmas in the City

We took rooms above the Fosters
    who'd also left the Cumberland
for a life away from mountains
    and we all tried the streetcars,

dime stores, brick-walled schools,
    learning what we had to, and well
before we knew it, December hung
    over us like a slack-looped garland.

'Don't worry,' said Mrs. Foster,
    'Christmas can come without a tree,'
and so it did, though I caressed
    the memory of nested ornaments back

in Grandma's attic. Santa and luck
    brought Father a factory job, for me
a line-up at the Vine Street theatre
    in a herd of displaced children

to watch 'Tom Sawyer' free and take home
    the dole of gift-wrapped peppermint;
we gathered round the radio, feasting
    on cured ham, buttermilk biscuits,

Silent Night Holy Night, and though I
    dreamed again of Hitler, his moustache
hoary and barbed, I conjured his
    demise in burlap, the sack tied

and hoisted up the chimney by elves.
    We all woke to the shimmer of rooftops
nestled one against the other
    across horizon's frost-slathered sprawl.

On Mobility

Small immigrant
from the mountains
she was unprepared
for anything like a city
anything like a city school
where little girls
wore pullover sweaters
and Poll Parrot shoes.

They knew
she could read
just as well as they could
but what about the dirt
under her fingernails
and that outlandish coat
from missionary rummage?

She learned
to suck out the dirt
while the Bluebirds
met for recitation,
removed the coat each day
two blocks from the iron gate;
it rode her right arm in.

All through the second grade
she was a princess
on tour in brown oxfords
carrying her own fine woollen train
into that red brick fortress
of inferiors.

Piano Lessons

Mother signed me up
though we had no piano
and Tuesday rolled around
three times a week, marching
me to Miss Lightburn's clutter
where a half-dozen of us
would plunk like E-flats
among the tubas and music stands,
listening each to the others
stumble over ancient keys
that got no rest from day's
first bell to last – 'There's a long,
long road a-winding,' 'Oh, Danny Boy,
the pipes, the pipes . . .'

Then came the day
we'd have to start practicing
at home; the finale for me,
happy at last to bow out –
no money for a piano, no room
in our upstairs flat –
but Mother figured a way
and I found myself seated
at the kitchen table
facing a cardboard keyboard.

I plunked out tunes
so full, so felicitous, that Mother
took up percussion – wooden spoon,
iron skillet, and when Father
got home, he'd have to coax us down
from 'On Top of Old Smoky.'

Looking at Skulls

The first skull I saw
     gleamed from a stereoscope
in Grandma's front room.

The scene was a Mideast catacomb,
     Jerusalem, perhaps, or Babylon;
Grandma favoured the Bible lands.

In three scoped dimensions
     two shadowy orbs leered at me
from a knob of chalky bone.

I scrambled for the next card –
     benign camels crossing the desert
or the sombre stillness of Golgotha,
     anything to squelch that deep vacancy.

Now, all these years later,
     I've met Hamlet and others
who do not turn from skulls;

I've lost Grandma
     whose hidden remains still comfort,
whose skull is surely beautiful;

and I've made peace
     with my own scaffolding –
femur, tibia, clavicle –

gliding me through this life
     like a fine ghost ship,
at sea with lofty captain

intent on solid grace,
     content with the usual gear:
nose, ear or two, eyes,
     the accoutrements of face.

Allies

From my attic window I'd look down on Mazuk's,
the storefront tavern across the street,
its hazy rituals of beer and song foaming

nightly in those heady weeks of 1945, soldiers
and sailors marching in to 'Roll Out the Barrel,'
dance all night, reclaim their back-home places.

Radio on and lights out, I'd sit on the floor
to catch the revelry my teetotaller parents never
joined, though their younger brothers – back from

Europe and the Pacific – were said to abandon
abstinence on the other side of town. Sweltering
beneath the rafters, I wrapped myself in cool

damp towels to witness the story of victory
and valour and lights going on again all over
the world. I was eleven, a child for whom war

was an exploding newsreel, flashing its sorrows
far from home. Then suddenly it was over,
the president saying the new peace would last.

Many wars later I stand with Japanese friends
among the folded cranes and peeled-off shadows
of their rebuilt city, ignited in 1945 by my

country's conjured sun. We climb the hills
that circle Hiroshima and, looking down, try
to imagine the cauldron of flame that raged below.

Enemies then, in child-ignorant spheres where
winning and losing were lessons apart, we stand
together now, our cinder hearts falling as one.

In Defense of Dark Woods

Can it be we fault the fairy tale,
that hard-edged story, fine respite
from the real fates around us?
Donald paddle-whipped for his lisp;

Roger collapsing below the blackboard
at the principal's announcement – his dad
dead in France; Hildegarde's big sister
sent away, pregnant at fourteen.

We children of the 'forties needed
an orderly justice to strew us a path
with breadcrumbs, parade for us
the lesser beasts beyond Truth's realm,

whisk us off to opulent balls to waltz
all night with a prince. The Grimms
gave us tangles and troubles and page-
turning pleasures, all raging in unearthly

spheres – wild, flat, inflating to fit
our imaginings; don't we still need that
vanguard of words, dream-stirred, prelude
to the journeys no one can spare us?

Swinging Bridge

A mountain begot my father and he never forgot.
 I still see us evacuating the city, crossing
the suspension bridge on a Friday, driving
 the slow hours back to the Cumberland.

My brother and I climb chalk-faced from the Nash,
 wobble along the Kentucky's dark bank
to the homestead's only portal,
 the swinging footbridge.

Father juggles the suitcases with new energy,
 Mother hugs her spice cake, saying,
'Don't look down,' and we inch along shifting
staves, gripping the long rope rail.

Midway over, the country uncles whoop inevitably
 aboard with thumping dogs and
grinning kids and one high ritual
 of rocking hugs.

Through night fog we cross muddy cornfields
 and inclined meadows first deeded
to Grandpa's grandpa, tree frogs singing
 for our ascension, and

my reserved father almost whistles at the sight
 of Grandpa waiting at the barnyard gate;
we climb on up to the porch, to the womenfolk
 and their ginger smells,

and at the helm of that high deck
 Father kisses his little round mother,
her face framed by white braids
 and mountain decades,

and she smiles at her first born, the first
 to go north, takes his hand,
and I know we have reached the other side.

21

The Porch

Back on the mountainside, my family joins
    Father's sprawling clan – a half dozen
of his sisters and brothers, their spouses

and broods – returned for a life-charging visit
    with the old folks, and all day we children
tramp the woods and wade the cold creeks.

Dusk comes early in the highlands, driving us
    and our hunger down past the orchard
to fried chicken and cornbread and the wide

gathering of grownups on the porch. There,
    in cricket-wrapped darkness, their talk
of city-dizzying lives hums around us,

rising and falling and later entering the windows
    to blanket us in our crowded beds: stories
of stiff factory bosses, heathen neighbours,

uppity store keepers, hawk-eyed landladies.
    Europe's war, Roosevelt, and our boys abroad
take other worrisome places in that litany,

but we kids sleep the easy sleep of the cared-for,
    waking at dawn to the aroma of coffee
and biscuits and that good rumble of voices

we'd gone to sleep to. Rising to eat again
    and meet the morning's admonitions – jam
on our chins, gingerbread in our pockets – we

line up at the porch edge, young paratroopers
    set to jump into the mists and passages of our
generation, the one that will lose the mountain.

On the Road with Betty Black

News of me, the city girl
down for the summer with old Miz Whitaker,
brings Betty racing in her daddy's red pick-up,
for which she is unlicensed, red dirt dusting
her red hair as she rolls along the unnamed,
unmapped, unpaved road, rattling her way
into the weedy yard, shaking the woodshed,
hen house, Grandma and me.

Fifteen and on her way to a life
she needs to imagine, Betty aims to get
herself a sidekick from sidewalks, a tutor
to throw some light on electricity and bath
tubs, dime stores and streetcars; through me
she'll glimpse that high-voltage world,
prepare herself for it, and in exchange
she'll steer me places in Pulaski County.

Me thirteen and trucking with
the spark-eyed Betty has Grandma worried,
but it's 1947, the war officially over,
soldiers back, and everywhere luck and hope
have shifted into high gear.

We cruise the pie suppers,
cake-walks, ball games, revival meetings –
the hard-driving Betty and me – spinning along
in freckling sun and sweat bees, starlight
and cricket song, she cozying up to field-brown
boys, me hanging back, not sure what our odyssey
means. I do, by summer's end, break a shy
heart or two.

But Betty breaks more, I later hear,
her urban dream cracking like a rammed
crankshaft the following May, when motherhood
settles into the driver's seat.

23

Mabel

She lived on the wall
in her white dress –

my mother's little sister,
framed in oval eternity
since her eighth year,

looking out over decades
at five brothers and six sisters,
their turbulence no bother,

so haloed in her dignity
that I'd stare long and deep
into eyes resting on somewhere else.

The spring I turned eight,
fourth grade had stiffened my soul
like rigor mortis, kept me

cringing at the blackboard,
wobbling on the gym mat;
but at day's end I'd go to Mabel,

study her ethereal hair
and will my scrawny spirit
to hang with her in refuge,

suspended in adoration,
our arms hooked, sweet as angels,
intent on our glassed-in vigil

where ceilings would never stop us
and our feet would never touch the floor.

Your Mother's Grandma

for Celia Mary Whitaker

One of your uncles, Roy or Clinton,
would drive her up from the country;
she'd step out of the coupe in snow,

a woman from another century, in ankle-
length skirts, thick stockings, bun-pinned
hair, and you'd have to change your ways

for weeks – share your room, likely your bed,
hide your lipstick, listen to hillbilly talk
of folks you'd never known or ceased to care about,

go elsewhere to meet your smart city friends;
but she'd grow on you, listen in ways no parent
could, tell you things that almost mattered, and when

it came time for her to go home, leaving water
spigots and light bulbs until the next time,
you'd help iron her aprons, wrap her one good

brooch for the suitcase, wave goodbye
from the driveway, and hurry upstairs
to cry your mixed-up emigrant eyes out.

She Who Waits

for Hattie Whitaker Dixon

On her youngest daughter's porch
    she keeps her vigil in bare feet,
        complains about the heavy biscuits,
lets her sojourning heart lift off
    to where it will – across the river
        to the homestead that still hugs
the mountain, occupied by strangers now,
    where kitchen, porch, springhouse and
        barn remain solid, breathing, heavy

like her own body; a place where dogs
    and horses, cows, chickens and hogs
        all had names; a place tangled in
memory like the long white hair she's
    tired of braiding. And she looks
        to another summit, dimmer, bluer,
nearer to Cumberland Gap, *Nearer My God
    to Thee*, where a piece-work graveyard
        holds the old settlers and their kin,

among them Dawson, lost within the year,
    lying beside a straggly rosebush no one
        remembers planting, its blood-tired
petals dropping on empty dirt, marking
    the place they'll be carrying her to –
        five sons, three sons-in-law, on foot
up the hill, twenty-six grandchildren at
    last count, Lord knows how many great
        grandkids; when life comes, it comes,

sure as it goes. All she needs now is
      the river, the mountains, the memory of
         Dawson's young hand warming hers as
they step off the footbridge, start up
      the 20th century. Meanwhile, she'll take
         a few more days of this earth's sky,
pouring its honey-sun across her toes,
      shelling its wild stars like sweet
         new peas across the darkness.

To Grandma, Out of Place

You have no business stretched out
wavy-haired in that lavender dress.

Not once in your eighty-four years
did you put on lavender,
did you curl your long hair.

Should you rise once more,
quit those satin pads and parlour roses
to go reclaim your proper kingdom,

the cows, lizards, cedars and stars
would not know you.

Dressing the Part

Lost to mirrors now, my mother
once filled them with her odyssey
of image. I frame her quest,

see the Great Depression lift,
the global war end, and Mother discover
the bargain basements. I see us ride

the streetcar down to Rollman's
where the Lower Level opens to a thick
bright catalogue sprung to life – blouses

in opulent tangles, seam-marked stockings
cascading from racks, wide neckties
flashing geometrics, crimson nightgowns

reeking of Rita Hayworth. We choose from the
Saturday mark-downs – rhinestones in dazzling
brooches, peasant skirts and saddle shoes,

fake fur collars and Dale Evans boots.
On the slow ride home I get the window
and a fat sack of caramels; Mother sits

square-shouldered, vainglorious as Joan Crawford,
and the shopping bag usurps the available floor.
At our housing project, Mother sidesteps mud

and reminds me we'll have a home someday,
a dozen forsythia bushes and a room for just me
with rosebud wallpaper and sit-down vanity.

I knew it to be true. Already she'd delivered us,
even my father, from the wilting mountainside
and the musty rooming house

ringed by soap factories; already she'd marched us, outfit
by outfit, through the city's dingy seasons, calculating
what it would cost

to qualify us for the elusive label
that takes a body anywhere,
makes a body somebody.

The Make-over

I'd set up shop in the kitchen
and go to work transforming my mother.

Patiently she sat, the only customer,
towel-draped in the chrome chair

while I, the child stylist, water-dipped
a long blue comb, ran it glistening

through her hair – that auburn waterfall,
thick waves cascading across my palm.

Forgotten were my own straw-straight
locks as I rolled and fluffed and patted

my client's, preparing her for
the kingdom ball where she'd put to shame

the frizz-domed stepsisters.
In those heady salon days, I imagined

a regal life for my country mother –
coiffed, ermine-robed, a Queen Elizabeth.

Later, when she claimed the lowly tower,
refusing to leave its homey walls,

I made her Rapunzel, hanging out
that astonishing hair; into it, she

could braid the world, draw in its fortunes.
Instead, she handed me the scissors.

Father's Friend

'Hunchy' they called him, no one
noting the burden of honesty
in that name. Father waited
on the porch for him every day,

and through the window I'd watch
as he turned up the walk,
his lopsided gait quickening,
homely features lifting

in a miracle of animation
beneath his dunsel cap, his spirit
straightening in ways his body
never could. Together they'd trod

the city blocks, carrying their
humped lunch pails to the factory's
rumble, to camaraderie among the lathes
of livelihood, rattling through

the night in those post-war years –
Hitler gone, Europe to rebuild,
America gearing up to run the world.
Then we moved to another neighbourhood,

Father took a better job, leaving
Hunchy to stumble with his bachelor
secrets past the fences, alleys,
railroad tracks, stepping off my curb

of memory. Until now, at the window,
thinking of my father long gone,
I see Hunchy's desert of loss,
share his cud of loneliness.

Machine Garden

for my Father

Among the steel cabbages
    in one of their rows
    away from the sun,
between two scarecrow lathes
        nestles a life
put there early to permanent place
    clamped in there
lower edges going to steel,
upper extremities oozing into gears
and the cold grasp of pinions;

small eyes stare out
the screw holes, worm holes
waiting for Sunday
and the ball game,
waiting for the weekend
down home in the mountains
to watch trees run free,
waiting thirty-five years
for a vinyl recliner
and a golden decade to watch TV.

The Uncles: An Album

Uncle Clay, the Holy Roller
married to square-jawed Helen,
stands in white suit and shoes,
New Testament in his pocket.

Uncle Rex, on the other hand,
can barely stand. Before prison
his spouse was the teary-eyed Una;
out of prison he courts a 300-pound
explosion named Daisy.

My mother's brothers line up
in memory, the pious and the damned –
a preacher's cast of rogues and saints,
sermons we've all had to sit through.

Blue-eyed Duke, Mother's favourite,
survived the beach at Normandy
to die in a 'fifties factory;
Roy, the scowling one, brought home
a peppered Mexican unwilling to blend;
and wide-bellied Clinton grew silent
with a wife who spoke in tongues.

Five maternal aunts led to five more
uncles – Raymond, Oran, Beckham, Castle
and Charles; and Father's four brothers,
Woodrow, Dewey, Steve, and Bill Dean,
plus three brothers-in-law, brought
a glut of seventeen uncles to watch
and learn from.

What I failed to fathom for myself,
the aunts confided to Mother,
and always I listened; what the aunts
didn't tell came from thirty-three cousins
hiding and seeking the family secrets.

My Kentucky uncles launched their careers
with the hand-held plow, lowered their dreams
into the man-eating mine, then abandoned
all that for the assembly line.

I saw them sell their days, horde their nights,
gracing and disgracing the bonds of family,
giving in at times, but not giving up.
And though we label their lot –
working class, hillbilly, have-not –

theirs was a brotherhood
that met its times, entered its places,
bequeathed its coterie
of lived-in faces.

Story Hour

Twice a month we marched down
the block to Miss Hamacher's
shelf-lined lair where Miss Hamacher
waited, open book in bony hand,
neck crooked, head extended, a benevolent
condor balanced for feeding her young;

first she'd smile, greeting
us through outsized teeth,
'Good morning, boys and girls,
welcome to the liberary' – a
sacred word, four syllables
that silenced our whispers.

Years later, as a teacher, I
took my class to the library
and there she stood, thin as
a bookmark, bent and poised
to launch Mary Poppins.

Lisa asked for a Judy Blume
book, one with divorced parents,
and Miss Hamacher looked down
from craggy decades, inhaled one
time, exhaled one time, and spoke
across the nested handkerchief
fanning from her bosom pocket:

> 'Boys and Girls,
> we are here to hear
> the *good* stories.'

Surviving Sweetie Jackson

There she is, the skittish new kid
                    oh, it's me
crossing the hopscotch court
thinking   *let me make it, please God,*
past the ten square, through the swings
across the project parking lot,
just one neat leap up the kitchen stoop,
then if she makes it, she'll edge
her breathless way into the pitch-dark pantry
                    safe at last.

I knew about Armegeddons in those days
(though I didn't call them that)
how they hid in stairwells, jumped
from hedges, rode your hapless heels,
how they . . .   *so did Sweetie catch up?*

Yes, yes, a thousand terrible yeses –
pudgy fists wedged, tongue pepper-tipped,
my terror airborne, her bravado heavy-
bottomed, a long seesaw of encounters,
ground-rupturing crashes.

Then spring, marking a half-year of up/down,
and something had to be done:
I'd have to take my place, *I'd have to Be.*

So look, that's me, clinging to my perch
on the monkey bars, a knock-kneed scrap
of determination, outhanging Sweetie's
shouts 'get down from there, you hillbilly,'
outlasting Sweetie's shin-raking fingernails,
and though it took a ragged month
                    I won the bars.

On to the teetertotter, across the
battlefield, and here comes truce,
Sweetie easing her commando bulk
after holding me aloft one thousand seconds
(Jimmy Watson did the count) and dignity

steps off with me somehow,
as I leave that dizzying seat – personhood
holding me erect all day and the next
and enough other days, year-meshed,
until at last I'm in communal country – *a citizen.*

The Sophisticates

for Patricia

The summer we were twelve
we climbed your attic stairs
to enter each day the swelter
we called New York.

Smart lady friends, we dressed
in lace curtains and long white gloves.
Our big time apartments
held cast-off mattresses, foggy mirrors,
lopsided chairs.

We danced with make-believe boyfriends
kissing them endlessly
at our imagined doorsteps,
never thinking to ask them in.

That was the August our classmates,
Joyce and Jeanette, ran off to Detroit
with two older guys, returning
with stories we couldn't believe.

Eighth grade started up
and we vacated New York,
but Detroit kept us
dangling for years.

The Slug

a week on the wall
and halfway up
the magpie spots him
another plump delicacy
this world provides
another slow odyssey
it interrupts

I think of Roger and a lineup along the gym wall – that
place of little progress, where we picked teams.
I see Roger's thighs, white as dumpling dough, puffy and
slow in regulation shorts; I hear a teacher summing up
Darwin: *some don't make it.*

the slug, unmindful
of theories and science,
sticks to naked truths,
luck and clinging,
though the snails somehow
drop with smug little shell-plops
to the tulip bed
as the drama of slug sacrifice
begins

How fiercely Roger must have clung – a soft lump of raw
hope, while the rest of us hardened in our shells; how he
must have prayed to the rope-hung ceiling, *Let someone
choose me, anyone, God.* I think how difficult, how dear,
for the species that climb.

Old Things, Gone Things

How hard it is to rid ourselves
of what has passed our needing –
old postcards, dried corsages,
monogrammed match books; we can't
give them up though we know
our loved ones will mutter
at the clutter we bequeath them.

My great grandmother's place
became *that damned rubbish heap*,
my uncles said, though I loved it
beyond all museums, sat dreamy
afternoons in the attic dwarfed
by yellowed papers, broken beads,
dusty hats, the trappings of a century.

When Grandma died, I'd moved
to a far city and no one was left
to covet her junk. My aunts
carried out two clocks, the carnival
glass, some hanging photographs.
The rest my uncles burned – house and all –
in the scant snow of a bleak countryside.

Even my mother's sparse treasures
were handed to others, somehow,
or hauled off in city trash.

I got her pearls and the company dishes,
but I miss the dime store vase
I bought her in 1943 and the peacock doily
she crocheted to save the one good chair
from my father's greased hair.

Item by item, my heart shelves
the inventory my hands cannot hold.

41

Book of Sunsets

Here is a page of afternoon
bound in winter's neutral hues –
black of tree, white of lake,
sheen of abalone sky;

I savour the stillness.

Too soon the clamouring sun
splashes its fuschia on the clouds,
crashes among the patient trunks,
calling up a time, decades and deaths ago,
when that same fat star rolled down,
tinting the pallid hills, staining the page
I did not want to turn.

Housewife

The slip covers
knew her heartbeat,
the linoleum
polished her knees;

but the wallpaper
can boast the most:
       she deflated one day
       still holding her feather duster
       and climbed flat
       into medallions
       and stylized peacocks.

It takes hours
to pick out her shape
as she lies in state
standing straight.

Six Strawberries

I wasn't ready to lose you;
that's why I wore cast-iron feet
for each of those visits
to your desert room,
to your hospital bed
in its quicksand of pain.

Your landscape was crimson,
the white walls shrieking,
I was astounded
you went on speaking,
you pulled large smiles
from a body so shrunken.

You finally stopped eating,
existing somehow on droplets
of will power;
but you broke that pattern
one afternoon in August
when I brought you six strawberries.

You ate the strawberries,
adding weeks to your life
and a hundred years to mine.

Miss Rinehart's Paddle

The long hard rumour
had hit us years before
but there was nothing we could do
to fend sixth grade off.
One September morning
we filed into Miss Rinehart's room
to face the thick glasses,
heavy oxfords, spit curls.

The weapon occupied
her middle drawer
and was rarely used on girls,
though Betty Jo got five whacks
for her haphazard map of Brazil –
the Amazon smeared and off-course,
Rio de Janeiro inland by inches.

I sat through six months
of imagined failures,
ended up a jittery stooge
with all 'A's,' the best parts in plays

and only now wonder
about the other side of power.

Meeting Geometry
for James Powell

Perhaps it was the classroom,
desks standing solid,
seats aligned with the
polished planks of truth;

perhaps it was the tools,
protractors leading hard-edged
journeys to precision,
glimpses of the absolute;

perhaps it was the teacher
bringing to his calling
a wire-rimmed integrity,
clear radius of caring;

whatever the particulars,
they all came together the year
I turned fifteen and ready for
the resolute science of angles.

To Delbert, Fellow Inmate, Grade Six

I'm sorry I sat there
halo bright, spelling words
down pat, report on Argentina
neatly stapled;

I'm sorry I sat there
hands folded, staring straight ahead
at the penmanship lesson
while old Miss Warren

dragged you up by your dirty red collar
cracking her paddle
on your corduroy bottom.
I knew you were just a crummy boy

who couldn't talk right,
your Daddy dead that year
and your Mom not making it.

I could talk right.
It's just that all my words
came from books and none of the books
were about skinny Delberts
with dead daddies.

Garnetta

. . . and then Garnetta arrived to
fracture the tedium of seventh grade math.
She manoeuvred her amazing figure to a desk

behind Clyde Barlow and no one
knew what to say. We'd learned to add
the occasional pupil, balancing our equation

one by one, but green-eyed Garnetta
and her cashmered torso contradicted our
straight line theorems and their connecting

points. We, the dull observers,
studied a string of high school suitors –
her company in the absence of curfew or father

or much-employed mother, while we
rode our bikes and held uneventful sleep-overs,
noting none of the minuses in young sophistication:

incomplete homework, failed quizzes,
abandoned childhood. Miss Pyle summed it up
at term's end – announced to the class

that Garnetta, 'a would-be Lana Turner,'
would star in a re-take; aiming the spotlight,
she welcomed Miss Turner back to grade seven.

We sat, the silent audience, satisfied
with the ways of justice, however scrawny, and no one
looked at Garnetta, though we all saw
the smudged mascara, the solitary tear. . . .

Forgiving the History Teacher

Our class did not hear
about Iroquois women who
owned the tribal lands
and thought for the tribe;
nor of Ann Hutchinson who
bypassed colonial clergy
and thought for herself.

We'd have grieved for
Massachusetts witches
had we known what truly
possessed them, for
plantation women whose
hymns through the cabin door
meant hauntingly more
than *quaint* and *southern*.

Miss Craig came to us buffeted
by her own skewed history –
Great Depression, global war
puzzle of spinsterhood.
She plotted progress
as a western story –
pale-skinned, turbulent, male –
the way she'd always heard it.

And though no girl could hope
to be George Washington,
she reasoned for us,
the nation could still use
some steadfast Marthas.

Inventing a Sister

She is missing,
always has been.
Yet I see her –
a grinning figure
seated between
my brother and me
on our fat swing of time.

Young enough
to think me a heroine,
old enough
to pick up the paper dolls,
she listens to my stories
endlessly, yawnlessly,
and doubles my wardrobe
as we change into puberty.

She flies home from Paris
to witness my wedding,
joins me in London
to celebrate my book.

When we grow inevitably old,
she outlives me.
I see her fine, wrinkled hands
sorting the photographs,
bundling the letters.

I slip smiling into her dreams
but always she wakes . . .
lifting slow, invented eyelids.

Father's Last Joke

I crank down his mattress,
dim the wall light.

'Can I bring you anything tomorrow?'

His head a small grey island
on the white sea of pillow,
face tranquil, the pain shored up.

I slip past an abandoned tray: still life
with cube of institutional cake,
brown plastic cup, sagging bent straw.

I kiss the distant forehead
as he kissed mine forty years ago.
In the hallway visitors click their exit
in outsiders' shoes.

I turn to leave.

'Wait,' his voice is scratchy,
clear eyes near.
Suddenly I ride out
in my old tire swing
feet thrust forward,
Daddy pushing, his blue eyes laughing.

'A chain saw.'

One pale foot eases
from beneath the sheet,
'I've got a terminal case of toenails.'

To a Pilot

in Southeast Asia, 1969

I know you
are still on it,
your bubble,
riding out
over smouldering fields
wearing your craziest hat.

But I can't look anymore.
Someone else is watching
from the earth below,
a man who didn't know you
when you were three
in a little blue sailor suit
trimmed in gold buttons.

The fields are his.

I will hurry, Brother,
to black and white headlines
every evening
to touch your altitude,

all the time hoping
your descent is gentle, is soon

before the spatter
of your bubble's rainbow,
the spilling of its stripes
moist among that man's crop
of burned out stars.

Leafing through the Album

I come across the photograph
that never failed to sweeten
my mother's face when she spoke
of 'her little girl.' Snapped

in a Kentucky field of high grass
the shot catches me kneeling,
my skinny arms bent
to the hoisting of an outsized

watermelon wedge. Although
the image is black and white,
I see the blue stripes
in my sunsuit, Mother's handiwork,

the pink of sun on my cheeks
and a glistening on my chin
as it fuses with the lavish red
of the fruit flesh. My eyes

beneath yellow bangs are bits
of sky widened by the juiciness
of the moment; and looking now
through the eyes of my mother,

a woman who scraped the pot
of scarcity, I savour this photo
as she did, re-live those feastings
on the mountainside, when summer

opened its good green rind
to us, and the next season
of diminishment had not yet
crept onto our vine.

Horizon's Hold

Of the million glimpses
this world gives you,
most slip quietly
to the mind's cold well;

but a few remain vivid,
tenacious, tattooing
themselves instead
to the warm inward eye.

Just so, I've kept the
landscape that gives me
back the child I was,
dreaming in a porch swing

up the mountain, marking
a bend in the Kentucky,
tracing its turbid flow
to the footbridge, rope-

hung, shimmying across
to the far side, to slopes
wading in blue fog, their
shawls patterned with sun.

The Magpies of Dublin

They have found me, scanned the dirtroads
and turnpikes of two American centuries,
working their way back across the sea
to these worrisome islands, to the crumbling
walls and tenacious moss they never forgot;
I should have known those emigrant women –
the great greats of aunts and grandmothers –
would grow curious about the not-yet-born
they never got to see, demand time out from
eternity for a swoop-forward genealogy.

Life came at them raw, relentless as hunger,
babies and choredom, riding the wagons
to Cumberland Pass and beyond; they staked
hill claims, scratched out hollows with pioneer
urgency, the Shawnee slipping tree-to-tree
bereft of welcomes in that dark and bloody
land. Polly, Hattie, Virgie, all free
of the blurred faces I studied in photogravure,
have come back – sleek-beaked, pecking among

the roof tiles, glaring at the neighbour's
cat, assessing my dusty windows
where lace hangs limp, their own white
aprons spotless. Peering in as I sit
at my writer's desk, they turn to chatter
in the maple, rendering me stiff and wordless;
at last they line up in guttural benediction,
silk heads dipping, weathered wings lifting,
and I rise to watch them choose the West.
Again the West. That gut-jostling passage.